Copyright © 2016 Debra Mastic

All rights reserved.

No part of this publication may be reproduced, distributed, or transmitted in any form or by any electronic or mechanical means, including information storage and retrieval systems, without the prior written permission of Debra Mastic, except in the case of brief quotations embodied in critical reviews and certain other noncommercial uses permitted by copyright law.

The information presented herein represents the view of the author as of the date of the publication. This book is presented for information purposes only. The views expressed are those of the author alone, and should not be taken as expert instruction or commands. The reader is responsible for his or her own actions. While every attempt has been made to verify the information in this book, the author does not assume responsibility for errors, inaccuracies, or omissions.

ISBN-10: 0-9980924-0-1
ISBN-13: 978-0-9980924-0-9

Contact Information: www.virtualresumecoach.com

LinkedIn is registered and trademarked by the LinkedIn Corporation. All uses within this book refer to the LinkedIn website and LinkedIn services provided by the LinkedIn Corporation.

Contents

Introduction	4
The Hiring Pipeline	6
Applicant Tracking Systems Uncovered	8
Creating an ATS-Friendly Resume	10
Optimizing Your Resume with Keywords	13
Resume Formats	16
Laying Out Your Resume	18
Resume Fonts	23
Things to Never Put on Your Resume	24
Career Summary	25
Current Employment Experience	28
Past Employment Experience	31
Optimizing Your Resume	32
Soft Skills	34
Hard Skills	35
Training and Professional Development	36
Education	37
Contact Information	39
Volunteer Work	40
Awards	41
Languages	42

Contents

Professional Affiliations and Memberships	43
URLs	44
Job Hopping	45
Employment Gaps and Unemployment	47
Career Change	49
Proofreading	51
Tailoring Your Resume the Fast and Easy Way	52
Applying for Jobs	55
Contact Debra Mastic	58

INTRODUCTION

When you're job hunting, there is a lot of pressure to write the perfect resume.

As a professional resume writer, job search expert, and founder of Virtual Resume Coach, LLC, I've had the opportunity to work with people in a wide range of industries and professions.

The same pain points surface for every person because resume writing sucks.

People don't want to be judged by their ability to write a resume, and very few people feel confident about their resume writing skills.

I have dedicated my career to understanding what makes resume writing so difficult. My goal has been to simplify the resume writing process so anyone can write a standout resume quickly and easily.

Resumes Made Simple is the resource that can do just that. For a fraction of the price of a professional resume writer, this book will provide you with an easy-to-use resume blueprint that gets results. I know you don't need a random collection of tips, you need a solution that is going to work.

What Makes Me Qualified to Write This Book?

I am not just a professional resume writer: I am an award-winning information design expert. People who work in the field of information design have a unique ability to:

- Communicate complex ideas with clarity, precision, and efficiency
- Collect, filter, and present information in accordance with effective design principles and cognitive psychology
- Design information for a specific audience to meet specific objectives

I am going to take a moment to expand on my last bullet. Think of writing a resume as designing information for a specific audience (recruiters and hiring managers) to meet a specific objective (get an job).

As a resume writer, my information design background gives me a unique advantage. I've spent years researching the hiring pipeline and interviewing recruiters and hiring managers to understand how they use resumes on a cognitive level. I've learned how to translate their needs into the perfect resume.

Over the years, I've heard the same feedback from recruiters and hiring managers: This is the best resume I've ever seen! It's because I figured out a process for creating an employer's dream resume.

How This Book is Organized

Having taught resume writing workshops to a wide audience, I have figured out how to break the resume writing process down into a resume blueprint—a simple design or pattern that can be followed to create an effective resume.

Resume writing is not a linear process for everyone and people don't list the same types of information on their resume, so this book is organized by topic. Everything you need to write your resume can be found in this book, from addressing employment gaps to creating an ATS-friendly resume to what type of font to use to a formula for writing the perfect summary statement... and so much more!

If there is a topic that you would like to see added to the book or if you have any questions or would like to connect with me, please contact me. Please visit my website www.virtualresumecoach.com or e-mail me at debra@virtualresumecoach.com. I would love to hear from you. I hope you enjoy this e-book. Thank you for reading.

Best of luck and thank you!
Debra Mastic

THE HIRING PIPELINE

The hiring pipeline is a process used by employers to narrow all of the people that apply for a job down to a small pool of final candidates. The hiring pipeline consists of three checkpoints to help employers manage and eliminate candidates efficiently because they don't have the time or resources to equally consider every person that applies for a job.

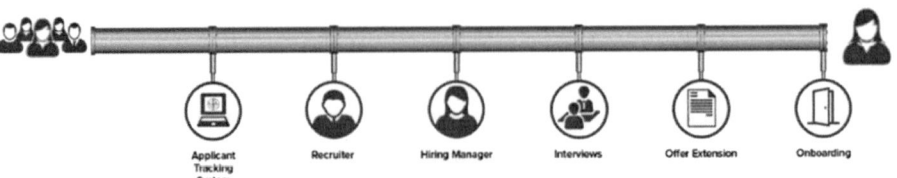

Checkpoint 1: Applicant Tracking Systems (ATS)

An ATS is an electronic tool that handles recruiting needs in order to make recruiters' jobs more manageable. Nearly all companies use some brand of ATS to handle job posts, store applications, and rank and track applicants.

Checkpoint 2: Recruiters

Recruiters are experts at scanning resumes and screening candidates to fill open positions. In most cases, recruiters are the company's first line of defense (i.e., they weed out the bad apples). Their goal is to make a good match between the candidate, the position, and the company.

Recruiters are:

- Analytical: They look for progressive experience and investments in your career. If you don't explain a gap or something that seems off on your resume, they will draw their own conclusions.
- Quick to judge: They are comfortable deciding to interview you or to pass on you after reading your resume for eight seconds or less.
- Skeptical: They are used to seeing lies, exaggerations, and half-truths on resumes and rarely accept anything at face value.
- Busy!

Checkpoint 3: Hiring Managers

Hiring managers are the people who requested for the position to be filled. Hiring managers look for people who can hit the ground running, bring new skills to the company, and mesh well with the existing team.

APPLICANT TRACKING SYSTEMS UNCOVERED

When you apply for a job, your resume gets stored in an applicant tracking system, or ATS.

An ATS is a type of software that helps recruiters manage resumes and applications. Think of an ATS as a search engine that can search through thousands of resumes because employers don't have the resources or time to equally consider every person that applies for a job.

While an ATS helps make the hiring process more manageable for employers, it makes the process of getting a job harder because there are no hard and fast rules about how to ensure your resume gets considered by a real person when you apply for a job.

Behind the Scenes of Applicant Tracking Systems

Have you ever wondered what happens to your resume after you apply for a job?

In most cases, your application and resume are stored in the database portion of a company's ATS. The user interface for each ATS varies by brand, but imagine your name going into a long list of applicants based on how you rank according to the recruiter's search.

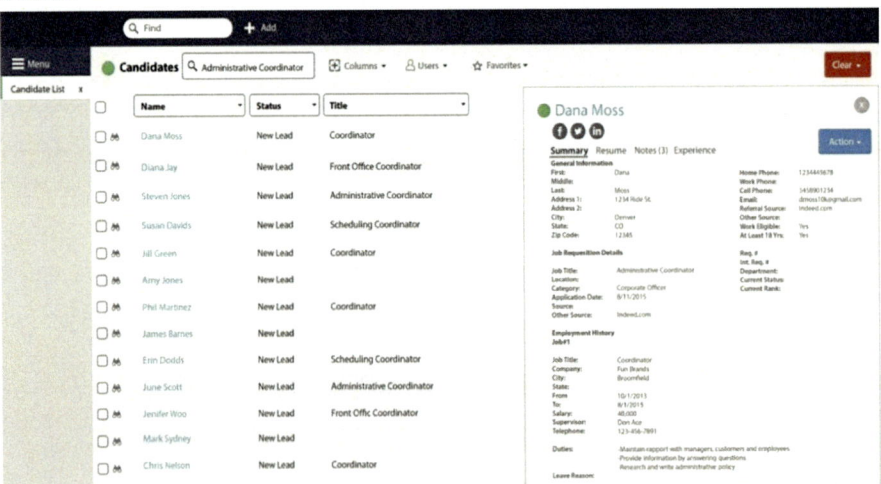

If a recruiter clicks on your name in the system, he/she will typically first see a bird's eye view of your application or profile, NOT your resume. If your application shows potential, he/she will open your resume for further consideration.

Imagine the recruiter seeing something like this (e.g., a basic form) after you complete an online application.

When I interviewed recruiters across the country to understand what they look for in online applications, they said:

- If the person has done the job they're applying for before.

- If the person is the right fit.

- If the person can be effective immediately. This means that little to no training is required and that the person's experience and skills align with the required skills and qualifications outlined in the job posting.

How you fill out the online application is just as important as submitting an effective resume. You need to input information that is relevant and tailored to the requirements and qualifications in the job posting.

CREATING AN ATS-FRIENDLY RESUME

There is no way to guarantee that your resume will be seen by a real person when you apply for a job. There are many factors that are out of your control, such as the size of the applicant pool, but there are things you can do to create a more ATS-friendly resume.

Use Relevant Keywords

The ATS is like a search engine for resumes. Recruiters use keywords to rank applicants because it would be a poor use of time to randomly review resumes without a filter.

While the ATS cannot determine if one candidate has better quality experience than another candidate, it can figure out who used the most relevant keywords in their resume. The more relevant keywords you have in your resume and application, the better you will rank in the search results.

Boolean Searches

Many recruiters use a Boolean search method to filter and rank candidates. Boolean searches involve using a string of keywords to find meaningful candidate results.

So, how do Boolean searches work?

A recruiter may use the search string "engineer AND quality assurance" to:

- Find quality assurance engineers.
- Eliminate manufacturing and operations engineers for a specific job opening.

If both keywords "engineer" and "quality assurance" are not found in an application, it will not rank in the search results.

For this reason alone, you should use the exact job title you're applying for in your resume and application because it is going to be one of the most relevant keywords.

If your job title differs from the job title you are applying for, use both job titles if appropriate. List your official job title followed by a comma followed by the job title that you are applying for. This will optimize your resume with relevant keywords while still being truthful about your formal title. You can also do this in the online job application. Here is an example.

WORK EXPERIENCE

Web Developer, Web Designer – Company Name, 2013 – Present

Let's review another example of a more complex Boolean search string.

A recruiter can use multiple keywords joined by "AND" or "OR" in a search string to find specific candidates.

For example, she could use the string: "helpdesk OR help desk OR technical support AND POS". In this string:

- The use of "OR" means she will accept any form of the keyword listed ("helpdesk OR help desk OR technical support") because all of those terms are interchangeable in the recruiter's mind.
- The use of "AND" means the application must include the keyword "POS" because the recruiter wants to find someone with POS experience. This is a non-negotiable keyword.

If your application and resume do not contain the right combination of relevant keywords, you may never be considered for the job because you will be filtered out based on the search string.

Formatting

The modern ATS has advanced parsing abilities so you do not have to submit a stripped down text document without formatting. There are, however, a few things you can do to help make your resume easier to scan.

- Use standard headers like "Work Experience", "Skills", and "Education".
- Put headings in all caps on your resume to help the ATS categorize your information.
- Avoid using headers and footers in the document.
- Upload your resume as a PDF unless otherwise noted in the application instructions.
- Do not use graphics on your resume.
- Use simple bullets and keyword characters (no special characters).

OPTIMIZING YOUR RESUME WITH KEYWORDS

Optimizing your resume with relevant keywords can help it rank higher in search results, which will significantly increase your chances of getting your resume seen by a recruiter.

If your resume ranks in the top 10 results of a keyword search, your chances of being considered by a real person are much higher than if your resume ranks lower. Recruiters want to start calling and interviewing people before they have to go through dozens of resumes.

Put yourself in their shoes for a moment. When you do an Internet search, wouldn't you rather click on the first couple of search results instead of the fiftieth search result?

How to Determine Relevant Keywords

Before optimizing your resume with keywords, you need to be able to accurately anticipate what keywords to use.

Job postings are misleading because responsibilities are typically listed above requirements. This gives the impression that you should tailor your resume to the responsibilities instead of focusing on how your experience aligns to the requirements listed at the bottom of the job posting. Responsibilities, however, are listed at the top of the job posting solely to give you an understanding of what the job involves.

Recruiters use keywords from the "Requirements" or "Qualifications" section to filter and rank candidates because if candidates do not have the basic requirements to do the job, the rest of their experience is meaningless.

In the sample job posting below, the keywords that recruiters would most likely use in a keyword search for the position are highlighted.

Why Are These Keywords Relevant?

Relevant keywords align with hard skills, not soft skills. Hard skills are demonstrable, experienced-based skills like being proficient in a software, being fluent in a language, or having a formal degree.

Relevant keywords rarely align with soft skills like "attention to detail" or "strong time management" because those skills are too subjective and will not produce meaningful candidate results.

How to Use Relevant Keywords in Your Resume

Now that you know how to identify relevant keywords that you can use to optimize your resume, let's talk about how to incorporate them in your resume effectively.

Recruiters and hiring managers do not put much stock in a laundry list of skills anymore, so try to avoid listing them like in the example below.

SKILLS

- Google Analytics
- SQL
- A/B Testing

For best results, use keywords and phrases in the context of your actual work experience. In the example below, see how "Google Analytics" is used in context instead of just being listed under a skills section. This is just one example, and it is not the only way to include a hard skill in an experience section.

Product Marketing Manager – Company Name, 2013 – 2016

- Implemented and managed insurance product marketing programs; used Google Analytics to communicate trends, monitor progress, and make plan adjustments

RESUME FORMATS

There are three main types of resume formats: functional, infographic, and chronological.

Functional Resumes

Functional resumes highlight your abilities instead of your work experience. Employers use your resume to get a clear picture of your career progression. Therefore, nearly all employers dislike functional resumes because people generally use functional resumes to hide employment gaps and frequent job gaps.

In the following example, the skills are listed by type of skill (e.g., management skills) instead of by job. The problem with doing this is that you tend to lose credibility when you do not list where you earned specific experience. In this example, the resume writer included a bullet point about supervising a staff of 10 people but doesn't associate the experience with a specific job, which makes the experience hard to verify.

> **Management Skills**
> - Supervised a staff of 10 people
> - Wrote and implemented new hire training

If you use a functional resume, many employers will discard your resume without a second thought.

Infographic Resumes

Infographic resumes visually communicate experience instead of using words. There are several problems with using an infographic resume.

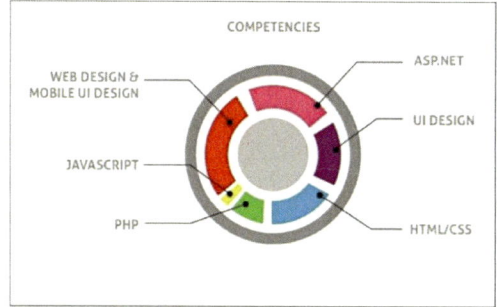

First, employers question candidates that emphasize style over substance. Your skills and experience should speak for themselves without the use of fancy charts or pictures.

Second, it is actually harder to comprehend an infographic resume. In this example, what the resume writer is trying to convey is ambiguous.

Third, graphics take up more space than words. By using infographics, you are saying less with more, which is the opposite of what you want to do on a resume. If you want to show off graphic design skills, include a URL to an online portfolio with samples.

Chronological Resumes

The most common type of resume is a reverse chronological resume which begins with your most recent experience and goes backwards. Each job gets its own space to highlight relevant skills, responsibilities, and accomplishments.

Using a reverse chronological resume is the best choice because recruiters and hiring managers want to get a clear picture of your career progression and what you are currently doing, even if your employment history is not picture perfect.

LAYING OUT YOUR RESUME

When it comes to resumes, many people do not know where to start, what to say, and how to lay them out because the process can be overwhelming. That is about to change thanks to this secret that makes the layout part really easy.

To create an effective resume, plan on laying information out in your resume in the same order that your resume readers (recruiters and hiring managers) are looking for it.

Unlike book readers, resume readers skim and scan resumes instead of reading them from top to bottom (or front to back). Do not expect them to read every word on the page. If you inadvertently bury important information at the bottom of your resume or in the middle of a dense paragraph, it will most likely be missed and not taken into consideration during the decision to interview you.

When you lay out your resume according to your resume readers' needs, the resume reader will be able to find what he/she wants to see as efficiently and naturally as possible. Since recruiters only spend eight to ten seconds scanning a resume before making a decision, it is best to anticipate what they are looking for and make those things easy to find in your resume.

How Employers Read Resumes

Employers do not expect to see a fancy-looking resume with pretty colors because they value substance over style. The best option is a resume that is clear, organized, easy to read and understand, and shows how your experience is a good match for the job.

When a recruiter or hiring manger opens your resume, they universally look at pieces of information in the following order:

- Your name
- Current employment (This is most important to them because they want to see if you are currently employed and what you are currently doing. All of the recruiters I interviewed for this book admitted they would rather interview someone who is currently employed over someone who is unemployed.)
- Past employment (to get a picture of your career progression or lack of career progression)
- Required skills and qualifications (those relevant keywords that show if you have the basic required qualifications listed in the job ad)

When you envision a resume, does something that looks like this come to mind?

NEHA MATTU
1234. Street Name, City, ST 11111
email@fakeemail.com   111.222.3333   www.linkedin.com/in/fakeprofile

MARKETING LEADER
Marketing Visionary and Goal-Oriented with a Proven Track Record of Achieving Desired Results

Creative, high-energy leader with a proven track record of successful projects from concept through completion. Exceptional relationship manager with collaborative abilities and expertise nurturing high-profile relationships in challenging environments. Talent for building cohesive teams with strong problem-solving skills. Adept at leading by example.

- International Marketing
- Team Building
- Customer Engagement
- Competitive Analysis
- Forecasting
- Digital Marketing
- Integrated Marketing Communications
- Pricing

PROFESSIONAL EXPERIENCE

COMPANY NAME
Marketing Director   2010 – 2016
- Spearheaded multiple concurrent product releases and established long-term partnerships with representatives and managers
- Planned and implemented concepts and promotional tours
- Collaborated with stakeholders to expand distribution in accordance with revenue and sales objectives while remaining within the target budget

COMPANY NAME
Marketing Manager   2000 – 2010
- Designed and implemented the 5-year marketing plan and managed the marketing mix
- Created an online campaign through multiple channels such as websites, blogs, social media and forums
- Drove a marketing strategy through multiple product launches
- Built innovative business-to-business research site in accordance with advertising policies

COMPANY NAME
Marketing Specialist   1998 – 2000
- Built the corporate identity and developed branding policies
- Implemented process improvements from feedback

EDUCATION
Bachelor of Arts (BA), Marketing; 1997
University of the World, City, ST

This resume leads with the person's name followed by her address, summary, skills, experience, and education. The problem with this common resume format is that it does not align with how employers read resumes.

First, recruiters and hiring managers do not put any stock in cliché summaries full of subjective terms like "results-driven, "high-energy leader" and "goal-oriented with a proven track record of achieving desired results" because those terms do not provide valid information. Just because you claim you are "goal-oriented" does not prove it.

These types of summaries actually come across as generic because they are so overused. Employers have been programmed to skip over homogenous summary statements because they do not provide useful information that can be used to make a good decision.

MARKETING LEADER
Marketing Visionary and Goal-Oriented with a Proven Track Record of Achieving Desired Results

Creative, high-energy leader with a proven track record of successful projects from concept through completion. Exceptional relationship manager with collaborative abilities and expertise nurturing high-profile relationships in challenging environments. Talent for building cohesive teams with strong problem-solving skills. Adept at leading by example.

Instead of using a subjective term like "strong problem-solving skills," recruiters and hiring managers would rather see an example of a problem you solved and the results under a specific work experience. Ideally, your summary should cover your unique selling proposition.

Below the summary in the resume, there is a list of skills. This is also very common in resumes. Like the summary statement, recruiters and hiring managers no longer put much stock in a skills section. They would rather see how you have applied the skills in your jobs (with context) than see them mentioned in a long list.

- International Marketing	- Forecasting
- Team Building	- Digital Marketing
- Customer Engagement	- Integrated Marketing Communications
- Competitive Analysis	- Pricing

The moral of the story is that you should not waste space on your resume with things that resume readers skip over just because you think a resume needs to look one way.

Effective Resume Layouts

Now that we have talked about why the most common resume format is ineffective, let's look at some alternatives. You can download the following resume templates from www.virtualresumecoach.com.

The Single-Column Resume

The most basic resume layout is a single-column resume. This format can work for anyone because it is so simple. The resume has lots of white space which helps provide clarity and legibility. Additionally, the subtle lines help compartmentalize and break up information, making it easier to scan.

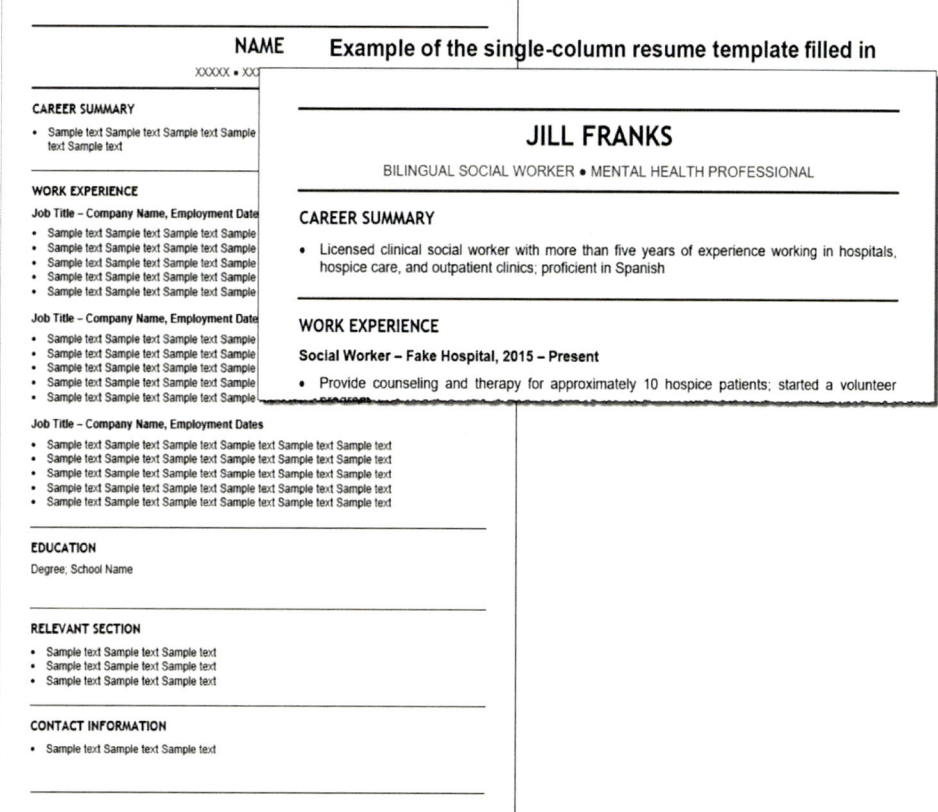
Example of the single-column resume template filled in

The Two-Column Resume

The two-column resume template enables you to put more types of information on the first page, as well as highlight skills, qualifications, and experience.

Example of the two-column resume template filled in

NAME
XXXXXX • XXXXX • XXXXXX

EDUCATION
Degree; Fake University

CERTIFICATIONS
Sample text
Sample text
Sample text
Sample text
Sample text
Sample text
Sample text

PROJECT HIGHLIGHTS
Sample text
Sample text
Sample text
Sample text
Sample text
Sample text

VOLUNTEER WORK
Sample text
Sample text
Sample text
Sample text
Sample text

CONTACT
111-222-3333
name@fakeemail.com
City, ST (Zip code)

CAREER SUMMARY
- Sample text text sample

WORK EXPERIENCE

Job Title – Company Name, Employment Dates
- Sample text text sample
- Sample text text sample
- Sample text text sample
- Sample text text sample

Job Title – Company Name, Employment Dates
- Sample text text sample text sample text
- Sample text sample text sample text sample text sample text sample text
- Sample text sample text sample text sample text sample text sample text
- Sample text sample text sample text sample text sample text sample text

Job Title – Company Name, Employment Dates
- Sample text sample text sample text sample text sample text sample text
- Sample text sample text sample text sample text sample text sample text
- Sample text sample text sample text sample text sample text sample text
- Sample text sample text sample text sample text sample text sample text

Job Title – Company Name, Employment Dates
- Sample text sample text sample text sample text sample text sample text
- Sample text sample text sample text sample text sample text sample text

JASON BARNES
SECURITY OPERATIONS • LEADER • MILITARY VETERAN

EDUCATION
BS, Business Administration; Fake University

CERTIFICATIONS
Hospitality Law
Hotel Security Management
Disaster Preparedness & Emergency Response

CAREER SUMMARY
- Senior leader with more than 10 years of experience in security operations in the hospitality industry
- Completed three tours of duty in Iraq; awarded multiple Army Achievement medals based on leadership abilities

WORK EXPERIENCE

Director of Security Operations – Hotel, 2014 – Present
- Manage security operations for a hotel with 500 rooms and approximately 1,500 employees and guests; supervise 10

RESUME FONTS

Wondering what types of fonts to use in your resume? You can use one of these fonts if you want to keep it simple.

Important: Your body font should be 12 points. It's tempting to use smaller font to fit more words on a page, but recruiters won't read your resume if the font size is too small.

Resume Body Font Choices
- Arial
- Garamond
- Cambria
- Calibri
- Times New Roman

Resume Header Font Choices
- Trebut MS
- Tahoma
- Verdana

THINGS TO NEVER PUT ON YOUR RESUME

If any of these things are in your resume, delete!

- Objective statement
- The phrase "Responsibilities included"
- References available upon request
- Irrelevant information
- Personal information including your marital status, age, street address, etc.
- Pictures
- Relevant coursework
- Dense paragraphs of text
- Subjective terms and statements
- A description of the company you work for
- Salary information

CAREER SUMMARY STATEMENTS

Even though you will see resumes with a career summary, they are not a must-have on your resume. Employers will not hold it against you if you skip a summary and dive right into your experience since your resume is technically a summary of your work experience.

Why Career Summaries Fail

Recruiters and hiring managers have been conditioned to automatically skip over career summaries on resumes because people have been taught to write them so poorly.

For example, the following career summary is ineffective because it is full of vague, cliché terms like "visionary," "proven track record" and "creative." It is actually painful and boring to read.

> **MARKETING LEADER**
> **Marketing Visionary and Goal-Oriented with a Proven Track Record of Achieving Desired Results**
>
> Creative, high-energy leader with a proven track record of successful projects from concept through completion. Exceptional relationship manager with collaborative abilities and expertise nurturing high-profile relationships in challenging environments. Talent for building cohesive teams with strong problem-solving skills. Adept at leading by example.

How to Write an Effective Career Summary

Your career summary should be short, authentic, and high-level. It can encompass:

- Years of experience
- The types of industries you have worked in
- The kinds of organizations you have worked for
- Special skills or designations that set you apart
- Your top unique selling points
- Your education credentials (if you do not have an "Education" section on your resume)
- Past experience that is relevant, but too old to list on your resume

Why?

Two common requirements you will find in most job postings are a minimum number of years of experience and experience in a specific type of environment (see example below).

> Required Skills/Knowledge/Experience:
>
> Impeccable front-end coding skills, imaginative, well-organized, good-natured, dedicated, agile and p
> in Computer Science, Multi-Media Design (or a related field), you have the following:
>
> - Strong development portfolio
> - ==2-4 years front-end development experience, preferably in an interactive agency==
> - High-level command of HTML, CSS, JS, JQuery, as well as basic knowledge of Photoshop.
>   - Experience with Drupal and React.js a huge plus!

By including your years of experience and what industries or types of organizations you have worked for in your career summary, you make it easy for your resume readers to find.

However, there are some rules when it comes to years of experience. If you have a lot of experience, round down just in case there is any hiring bias. For example, if you have 20 years of experience, say "more than 15 years of experience" on your resume. However, if you do not have a lot of experience, do not round up.

Here is an example of a career summary statement that would be effective for the job description above. It also includes a unique selling point (the mention of the national award).

CAREER SUMMARY
- Award-winning front end developer with more than five years of experience working in interactive agencies and startups; recently nominated for a national design award based on innovative design and quality coding

Career Summary Examples

If you are struggling to come up with your career summary, review these sample career summaries for some inspiration.

- Certified project manager with more than five years of experience managing software implementation and migration projects for startup companies; previously worked as scrum master for one year
- Bilingual paralegal with more than four years of experience working in immigration law and previous experience as an immigration social worker
- Registered nurse (RN) and certified nurse anesthetist (CRNA) with over five years of experience working in emergency, intensive care, and neonatal units

CURRENT EMPLOYMENT EXPERIENCE

Your actual work experience is the core of your resume. Your work history is the first thing employers look for on your resume, and it can weigh heavily in their decision to interview you or not.

Writing about your job can be difficult because it is hard to filter everything you do at your job into a few short bullet points.

The other problem is that most people have a tendency to unintentionally leave out important details and context because they are so close to their own experience. Something that makes sense to you on your resume may not always make sense to an outside reader.

My simple system will help you write your experience so your resume stands out. This is not the only way to write about your experience, just a good starting point.

How to Write Your Current Work Experience

Since your most current experience has the most significance on your resume, you can plan to write four to six bullet points about your most recent job.

Employers want to understand what you do at your job, as well as get a sense of your accomplishments. Each bullet point under your work experience needs to be clear so that anyone can understand what you mean.

It is also important to use your own words. There are lots of well-worded resumes on the Internet that you can copy and blend with your experience, but it is better to be original so that your resume stands out.

HOLD SHELF SLIP
Edmondson Pike Branch

Customer #: 5789

Item Number: 35192094443185
Title: Life of the party /
Placed on Hold Shelf: 9/5/2018

HOLD FOR:

MORELAND BOBBIE MARIE

Pull Date: 9/13/2018

In the first bullet:

1. List your core job responsibility while detailing the scope of your work.
2. Optimize your core job responsibility with a related accomplishment.

Core responsibility (including the scope)

> **General Manager – Store Name, 2015 – Present**
> - Manage the daily operations of a high-volume anchor store with multiple product categories and 80 employees; currently ranked 3 out of 150 stores based on revenue and gross margins

Accomplishment

In the second bullet:

1. List a secondary core job responsibility that is related to the job you are applying for.
2. Optimize it with a related accomplishment.

Core responsibility

> - Hire and train new employees; increased retention by implementing weekly engagement surveys

Accomplishment

In bullets 3-6:

List additional accomplishments. Employers know that certain responsibilities are associated with job titles so you do not need to list too many generic responsibilities.

- Selected to participate in a high-potential leadership program created for the top 5% of company managers; learned how to identify, duplicate, and nurture high-performing behaviors
- Created and facilitated PowerPoint presentations on merchandising strategies in multiple districts; selected by regional leadership to mentor other store managers on a monthly basis
- Improved the store's mystery shopping results by 15% in 2016 by implementing and communicating a rewards system that recognizes employees who provide great service

Remember, accomplishments are not just about winning a big award. An accomplishment can be exceeding a duty, improving a process, taking the initiative to fix a problem, taking on a new responsibility, receiving praise or recognition, being selected for a special project or committee, etc.

Top-Performing Resume Writing Tips

- Do not use periods at the end of your bullet points. This is unnecessary since you should use incomplete sentences in your resume.
- Do not just list generic job responsibilities. Optimize your responsibilities with measurable accomplishments.
- Do not use robotic, vague, or unclear language. Mirror the language in the good resume examples featured in this e-book.

PAST EMPLOYMENT EXPERIENCE

When writing about your past experience, know that employers really only care about your past 10, maybe 15, years of experience. Employers like to have a clear picture of your career progression, but the older a job is, the less relevance and significance it has on your resume.

How to Write About Past Work Experience

Here are the rules for writing about past jobs on your resume:

- Use past tense (e.g., "wrote" not "write" or "managed" not "manage").
- Convey your core responsibilities and accomplishments.
- Include two to four bullets of information for each of your past jobs.
- Do not go too far back in your work history. Going back 10 years is a good rule of thumb.

Here is an example of a past job written in past tense. It highlights a mix of responsibilities and accomplishments.

Lead Programmer – Bytes, 2012-2014
- Wrote manufacturing programs; debugged entry screens for the release of the company's main product
- Developed customized software solutions; received 100% customer satisfaction scores across 10 projects in 2014
- Promoted to the lead programmer role within six months; oversaw development, testing, and version control tasks

OPTIMIZING YOUR RESUME

Optimizing the bullet points in your resume means making them as effective as possible. Since you don't have lot of space on a resume, make every bullet count to really stand out. Here are three easy ways to optimize your resume.

Optimize Responsibilities with Accomplishments

Employers know that certain core responsibilities are associated with job titles. If your resume reads exactly like the job description, it won't stand out. When you can, qualify a responsibility with a related accomplishment.

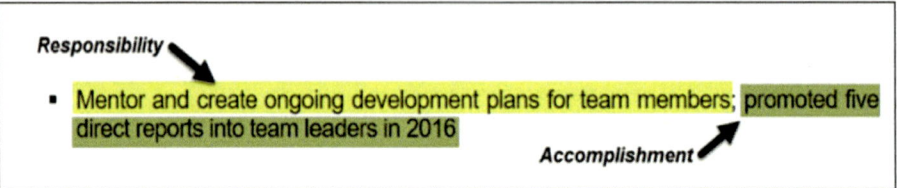

Optimize Accomplishments

Accomplishments are great, but they will be more meaningful if you explain how you achieved the accomplishment and how it made an impact on your organization.

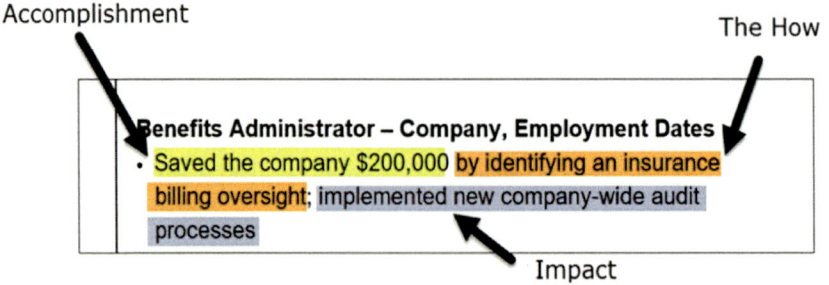

Bold Keywords

If you want something to stand out in your resume, use bold. However, know that if you bold too many things, nothing will stand out.

In the example below, the task is not relevant to the job (processing manufacturing orders). However, the ability to use attention to detail on the job was important so it was bolded to stand out.

- Process manufacturing orders; **use attention to detail** to follow complex order instructions

SOFT SKILLS

Soft skills are personable attributes that enable you to work effectively with other people. Soft skills include things like communication, interpersonal skills, teamwork, and problem solving.

Listing the words "effective communicator" or "problem-solver" on your resume is not going to add value because the employer cannot just trust that your self-assessment is accurate.

How List Soft Skills on Your Resume Effectively

For best results, talk about how you demonstrated soft skills in your work experience.

Let's say you are a strong negotiator. How do you communicate this on your resume? In this example, the resume mentions a specific negotiation experience and includes details on how the resume writer closed the deal.

- Successfully negotiated a large commercial contract work $5 million; adapted service level agreements and resolved perceived software issues to close the deal

Here's an example from my personal experience. This is a great example because my peers nominated me for a prestigious award and talked about my soft skills.

- Nominated for the Team Member of the Quarter in 2015; described by peers as a "dream co-worker" in the nomination

HARD SKILLS

Hard skills are provable, experienced-based skills like having a degree, software proficiency, and language proficiency.

Your resume should convey hard skills mentioned in the "Requirements" or "Qualifications" section of the job posting. In the following example, different ways to incorporate hard skills into a resume are highlighted in yellow.

Notice that you are not limited to listing hard skills in a formal skills section. You can embed them in different ways in your resume.

TERRELL JONES

PMP • PROGRAM MANAGER • CONSULTANT

EDUCATION

BS, Business Administration; University Name

Six Sigma Certificate; University Name

SKILLS

Microsoft Office Suite

Agile Certified

CAREER SUMMARY

- Senior project manager with more than 10 years of experience working in healthcare; active member of the Mile-Hi (Denver) PMI Chapter

WORK EXPERIENCE

Director of Security Operations – Hotel, 2014 – Present

- Manage the implementation of new HMO and health plan products; use Microsoft Project daily to create projects and manage tasks
- Developed and launched new PMO processes to 10

TRAINING AND PROFESSIONAL DEVELOPMENT

Constant learning is critical to your career success. Training and professional development can be assets on your resume because they show you are continually learning and developing yourself. Think of professional development as an investment in your career because you can take what you learn and apply it in your next job.

However, many people forget to keep track of their professional development, which means it gets left out of their resume. Professional development could include attending workshops, online classes, webinars, networking, a mentorship, among other things. For best results, keep track of what you learned from each professional development experience so you can clearly articulate it if asked.

How to List Professional Development on Your Resume

If you have significant professional development, you can make it its own section on your resume like this. Note how each bullet includes details and context.

PROFESSIONAL DEVELOPMENT

- Franklin Covey Project Management Essentials; certified in Project Management Institute tools and standards in 2016
- 2016 IT Expo Conference; collaborated with other IT professionals and gained insight into big data and cloud security trends

---

You can also embed it under your work experience if the training was significant. However, if you attended one webinar, it might not be worth noting in your "Experience" section.

- Selected to participate in a high-potential leadership program created for the top 5% of company managers; learned how to identify, duplicate, and nurture high-performing behaviors

EDUCATION

Education is typically a requirement for most jobs, so you want it to be easy to find on your resume. Here are some basic rules you can follow when listing education on your resume.

Rules

- If you have a college degree, omit high school diploma information.
- If you have multiple degrees, put your most advanced degree first. For example, if you have a master's degree, prioritize it higher than a bachelor's degree.
- Omit your graduation date and year because employers cannot make a hiring decision based on the year you graduated.
- You can include special honors and your GPA, but employers do not care about that information unless you are in the higher education field.
- If your degree is still in progress, add an expected completion date.

How to List Education on Your Resume

Below are some examples of how to write your education on your resume.

- HS Diploma; High School Name
- BS, Economics; College Name
- Bachelor of Science in Economics; College Name
- Bachelor's Degree in Economics; College Name
- B.S., Economics; College Name
- B.S., Economics; College Name (expected completion June 2017)
- BS, Economics in progress; College Name
- M.A. Education; College Name

Where to Put Education on Your Resume

There is no rule about your education having to be a certain place on your resume. In the resume sample below, the education information has been placed in different locations and has been written in three different ways to show you some options.

KELLY CLINE
CERTIFIED PMP • PROGRAM MANAGER • B.S. BUSINESS ADMINISTRATION

EDUCATION

BS, Business Administration; University Name

Six Sigma Certificate; University Name

CAREER SUMMARY

- Senior project manager with more than 10 years of experience working in health care
- Bachelor's Degree in Business Administration

WORK EXPERIENCE

CONTACT INFORMATION

When listing contact information on your resume, list your phone number, e-mail address, and your city, state, and zip code. You don't need to include your physical street address on your resume.

CONTACT

111-222-3333
name@fakeemail.com
City, ST (Zip code)

VOLUNTEER WORK

Volunteer work can be great for your resume and career. It can help you learn new skills, gain professional experience, and discover hidden talents that could lead to finding your dream job.

Non-profit organizations never have enough help because few people can volunteer on a regular or even part-time basis. This creates a lot of opportunity to try out something new without risking your career.

For best results, convey volunteer responsibilities and accomplishments in the same manner you would for a paid job. Do not minimize your experience or leave out details just because it is unpaid experience.

Bad

VOLUNTEER WORK

- Volunteer for the animal shelter five hours a week

Good. This is an example of my personal volunteer work experience.

Spokesperson
Colorado Pug Rescue   2013 – Present
- Correspond with media outlets and communicate with the public on behalf of the rescue; appeared on CBS News Denver at the annual Pugly Holiday Sweater Party
- Write press releases, social media content, and articles to promote the rescue; published in *A Sheltered Life*, a magazine that promotes pet adoption
- Coordinate and run fundraising events and campaigns; raise approximately $5,000 for the rescue on an annual basis

AWARDS

Awards can enhance your resume as long as they are relevant to the jobs you are applying for. If you are working in the corporate space, an award for being the best goalie in your soccer league may not have a lot of impact on your resume.

How to List Awards on Your Resume

When listing an award, providing additional details can help enhance the significance of your award. Briefly describe the award in the same way you would tell someone about it who had no idea what you were talking about. You can include things like the:

- Date of the award (if recent)
- Significance of award (e.g. why did you win the award)
- Scope of the award (in your department, company-wide, national, global)

In this example, the awards are listed in their own "Awards" section with no additional context.

AWARDS

- President's Club Award
- Manager of the Year

Now see how providing some additional detail (the date, significance, and scope) makes the award so much more impressive and impactful.

AWARDS

- **President's Club Award**; based on being in the top 2% of the company for store sales and profit in 2016
- **2016 Manager of the Year**; selected by executive leadership from a pool of 500 managers

LANGUAGE PROFICIENCIES

No matter what type of job you are applying for, being bilingual is an impressive skill to highlight on your resume.

Qualifying Language Skills

If you can only speak a language, use the term "fluent".

If you can speak, read, and write a language, use the term "proficient".

Listing Language Proficiencies on Your Resume

You can list the proficiency in a "Career Summary" section.

CAREER SUMMARY
- Paralegal with over four years of experience working in immigration law and previous experience as an immigration social worker; ==proficient in Spanish==

You could also include it under a "Skills" section.

==SKILLS==
- Fluent in Spanish
- Proficient in French

You could also include it under an "Experience" section.

Translator – Company Name, Employment Dates
- ==Use proficiency in Spanish and French to== facilitate translation services between doctors and patients; recognized for being able to effectively communicate with people of all levels

---

42

PROFESSIONAL AFFILIATIONS AND MEMBERSHIPS

A professional affiliation is any organization or group that you belong to based on your profession.

Professional affiliations can look good on a resume because they offer members continued education and training programs, career development, and professional networking opportunities.

If you list a professional affiliation on your resume, make sure it is current. Do not list it if you are not currently a member.

Also be aware that you may be asked about your level of involvement in the group if you get an interview. If you are part of an affiliation, but you do not take advantage of any professional development opportunities, it would look bad to admit that in an interview.

There are several ways to list professional affiliations on your resume. If you are a member of multiple affiliations, consider creating a "Professional Affiliations" section. In the example below, the information in parentheses expands on some of the membership benefits of that organization.

PROFESSIONAL AFFILIATIONS

- Women in Technology (membership includes monthly career sessions and networking opportunities)
- Association of Information Technology Professionals (AITP)
- Association for Women in Computing (AWC)

If you are part of only one professional affiliation, you could mention it in the "Career Summary" section like this:

CAREER SUMMARY

- IT leader with 10 years of experience working in the telecommunications industry; member of Women in Leadership since 2013

URLS

URLs can help enhance your resume and establish your credibility. For example, if you say you have great graphic design skills, you can link to samples of your work. If you say you have great written communication skills, you can link to an article you have written.

Recruiters often do an Internet search on candidates, so they enjoy when a candidate leaves a web trail on their resume as long as it is not overdone.

Types of URLs

Below is a list of URLs that you may want to list on your resume. I do not recommend using too many URLs on your resume, just the ones that make a significant impact.

- LinkedIn™ profile (as long as it is robust and matches what you have on your resume)
- Professional website
- Portfolio
- Professional Blog
- Award Announcement
- Publications

How to List URLs on Your Resume

There is no one way to include URLs on your profile. You can consider making them a hyperlink, but they will be useless if your resume is printed. Here is an example of how to list a URL on a resume.

CONTACT INFORMATION

111-222-3333
name@fakeemail.com
City, ST (11111)
www.linkedin.com/fakeprofilename

JOB HOPPING

Job hoping is not as taboo as it used to be. In today's job market, it is common for people to work for a company for a year or less before moving on.

Some recruiters and hiring managers consider length of employment at each job when screening candidates, but many are willing to take a risk on people who have the right experience and skills because they have an open position to fill.

When I relocated from Michigan to Colorado for a new job, I had recruiters contacting me about job opportunities the moment that I stepped foot in Denver. They did not care that I had just relocated for a brand new job because they were very interested in my experience and skills.

How to Address Job Hopping on Your Resume

If you held a job for less than a year, consider using these strategies on your resume to help put recruiters and hiring managers at ease.

Note: Many sources will tell you to address your reason(s) for job hopping in a cover letter, but the problem with that is the majority of employers do not read cover letters anymore.

Explain the Reason

If you changed jobs frequently because of reasons out of your control (i.e., downsizing, job elimination, spouse relocation, etc.), list it subtly on your resume.

For example, if you were downsized, relate your situation to poor economic or financial conditions (if possible) instead of slandering your past company. If you were dismissed (fired) for a specific reason, you will have to wait to explain that until the interview. Do not list the reason on your resume.

In the example below, the reason for leaving has been added in parenthesis after the employment dates without using negative words like "laid off" or "downsized", and it has been related to an economic downturn.

Surveyor
Company – *Tenure shortened due to an economic downturn*   2016
- Researched and collected survey data; established maps

If you left a relatively new job for a better opportunity, subtly emphasize how the quick job change was a great opportunity.

In the example below, the wording "recruited" has been used to communicate that he was not actively looking for jobs and to explain how the change benefited him (he got the opportunity to participate in a leadership development program).

Assistant Manager – Company Name, April – Present
- Manage daily call center operations and supervise a staff of eight customer service representatives; recruited to participate in a high-performing leadership training program

---

Use Years Instead of Specific Months

Instead of listing months and years on your resume, just list years for each job. Most employers do not care if you only use years. Keep in mind that you may be asked for the exact months in an online application, so it is important to provide specific information when requested.

Assistant Manager – Company Name, 2014
- Manage daily call center operations and supervise a staff of eight customer service representatives; recruited to

EMPLOYMENT GAPS AND UNEMPLOYMENT

Unemployment happens. However, just because you are unemployed does not mean you cannot work and stay fresh. Here are some things you can do to keep your resume current while you are unemployed.

Do Meaningful Volunteer Work

Volunteer using your core skills. If you are a web developer, volunteer to build or update websites for non-profits.

Web Developer
Denver Food Pantry   2016 – Present
- Updated the visual design of the organization's website; optimized web assets for optimal speed and performance

---

Do Freelance Work and Consulting

You can set up an account on Freelancer.com or Upwork.com and take on individual projects while looking for work. However, you cannot just say you have done consulting on your resume. You need to provide details and specifics like in the example below.

Freelance Graphic Designer   2016 – Present
- Designed a logo and marketing brochure for a private client; received a 100% client satisfaction rating on the project

---

Do Professional Development

Many employed people have a hard time balancing work and professional development because it seems like there is never enough time to do both.

Take advantage of your free time to do as much professional development as possible because it helps show that you are still engaged in your profession and adding new skills to your tool belt.

There are a lot of free opportunities if you cannot afford to pay for anything. Professional development can include webinars, workshops, online and in-person classes, certifications, and more.

Addressing Employment Gaps

It's true. The longer you have been out of work, the less desirable you are to employers. Employers would rather hire someone who is currently employed over someone looking for work because they are fresher.

If you do not address why there is an employment gap on your resume, employers will be forced to make assumptions. The only thing you can really do on your resume is explain the gap. Employers will be more understanding if there was some intention to the gap like in the example below. In normal circumstances, there should be no mention of personal family or marital status details on a resume.

PROFESSIONAL SUMMARY

- Group fitness trainer and personal trainer with five years of experience working in fitness and recreational centers; ==temporarily left the field in 2013 to prioritize family needs==

If you went on a sabbatical, make sure you say it was a planned sabbatical if possible. It's also good to explain how you were productive during a sabbatical.

If you were fired, you do not want to put that on your resume. You only need to put start and end dates on your resume.

CAREER CHANGES

In today's competitive job market, it is difficult to get noticed, even when you have the right experience. When you are changing careers, you may run into difficulty getting hiring managers to take a chance on you. And who can blame them? Why should they pick you over people with more relevant experience?

When you are applying for a job you have never done before, you cannot use your old resume. You need to determine which of your current skills and responsibilities transfer and emphasize them in your resume.

For example, you may want to create a table where you list out the requirements and qualifications required for the new career path. Then match your relevant experience to the list so you know what to emphasize in your resume.

For the qualifications that you lack, you should determine an action plan to gain the skills.

Here is an example of a detention officer who wanted to change careers to an entry-level investigator.

Requirements and Qualifications	Relevant Experience
Investigative Interviewing	Conduct investigative interviews following major incidents (e.g., fights, stabbings and murders) to identify instigators
Writing Reports	Write reports and memos used as evidence in court
An ability to handle emergency situations	Announce emergency and crisis situations and issue keys and emergency equipment to staff
Crime Scene Processing	Action Plan: Take formal training in crime scene preservation techniques and volunteer for the Citizen's Academy at the police station

Preparing for a Career Change

To help your career change go more smoothly, consider trying one of these strategies to build your resume.

Do Volunteer Work
One of the best ways to build your resume for a career change is to do volunteer work to gain relevant experience. There are plenty of high-profile volunteer roles where you can build credible experience. Just make sure to properly document and keep track of your volunteer work if you are going to substitute it for formal education or experience.

Ask Your Company for Help
If you are currently employed, let your employer know you are interested in learning a new skill or job. Ask if you can shadow someone already doing the job or take on related projects to build your resume.

Do a Formal or Informal Internship
A formal internship is usually a good way to get your foot in the door. If you do not have time for a formal internship, consider doing an informal internship. An informal internship may be a non-paid experience that you initiate and manage, shadowing someone informally or working on projects as you can.

PROOFREADING TIPS

Before you apply for a job, always proofread your resume.

- Have another person proofread your resume because your brain has a tendency to fill in the gaps and correct errors.
- Take a break before your proofread your resume. You will catch more mistakes with a fresh pair of eyes.
- Print out your resume and read each line out loud. If you wrote something incorrect or awkward, you will notice it when you read it out loud.
- Look for common errors such as spelling, grammar, punctuation, capitalization, verb tense issues, and weird formatting errors.

TAILORING YOUR RESUME THE FAST AND EASY WAY

You have probably heard that you need to tailor your resume to each job you apply for, but resume templates never seem to come with instructions on how to tailor your resume to a job.

Why Tailor Your Resume?

Tailoring your resume for each job posting does take more time, but it is totally worth it. In today's competitive job market, quality is more effective than quantity because employers do not bite on one-size-fits-all resumes anymore.

Busy recruiters spend less than ten seconds scanning a resume, so to stand a chance your resume needs to clearly show employers why you are a good match for a job. If you do not seem like a good fit upon first glance, they have no problem moving on without a second thought.

When you tailor your resume to a job, you are going to be perceived as a more qualified candidate and have a much better chance of getting an interview.

How to Tailor Your Resume

Step One
Identify the requirements and desired qualifications in the job posting and optimize your resume with the same specific keywords and wording used by the employer. Changing "lean manufacturing" to "lean production" or "user-centered design" to "user experience" may seem subtle, but these changes can have a big impact.

Recruiters are not always experts in the field they recruit in, so they look for certain keywords on a resume to figure out if someone is qualified for a position.

Step Two

Make the requirements and qualifications easy to spot in your resume. Recruiters are busy and only spend eight to ten seconds scanning your resume before making a judgment about you. Do not inadvertently bury important information based on the faulty assumption that recruiters will read every word on your resume.

Here is an example of highlighting an important qualification (PMP). It is highlighted under the applicant's name, the most focal part of her resume.

JASMIN WILSON
PMP • ACTIVE SECRET CLEARANCE • CONSULTANT

EDUCATION

Bachelor of Business Administration; Fake University

SKILLS

Microsoft Office
Microsoft SharePoint
SQL

CAREER SUMMARY

- Project manager with more than five years of experience working in PMO departments; previously consulted and managed projects for Fortune 500 clients

WORK EXPERIENCE

Project Manager – Company Name, 2015 – Present
- Manage large-scale infrastructure upgrade projects; develop project plans and oversee project teams.

Step Three

Cut irrelevant information and replace it with relevant information. Do not be afraid to swap out pieces of your experience and skills based on the job you are applying for.

If you were applying for a technical writing job in the health care industry from the ad below, you would emphasize any related health care, clinical, and research experience because it is called out in the job requirements.

Qualifications:

- Bachelor's Degree in Technical Writing, Health Informatics, Computer Science, health-related field or similar.
- Three years' experience in technical writing and training.
- Professional relevant experience, in addition to the required experience, may substitute for the bachelor's degree on a year-for-year basis.
- This position will be within the Research Institute and will interact with clinical and translational researchers.
- In addition to technical experience, experience with research regulations is preferred.
- Experience in health care or with health care data is preferred.
- Prefer Master's degree.

However, if you were applying for a technical writing job in a more technical industry as in the following ad, it would not make sense to emphasize any health care experience because it is not relevant to the job requirements.

Requirements:

An associate degree in English, Technical Writing, Journalism or Engineering preferred.
Excellent verbal and written communication skills (4+) years' experience writing technical or business documents.
Advanced knowledge and use of MS Office tools (Word, Excel, PowerPoint, and Visio).
Experience using Atlassian applications (primarily JIRA and Confluence) and test case management tools preferred.
Experience with front-end technologies, such as JavaScript, HTML5, CSS3, and Wiki Markup preferred.

Both jobs require the same foundational knowledge and skills, but it would not make sense to use the same resume to apply for both for jobs.

APPLYING FOR JOBS: HOW TO GET A RESPONSE

You probably already know how to apply for a job. You go online, fill out the application, and upload your resume.

To increase your chances of getting a callback, use my top-performing tips when applying for jobs.

Top-Performing Tips

Complete the Application Legibly and Completely

When you do not have a lot of extra free time or you are sick of applying for jobs, it may be tempting to get a little lazy when filling out the online application, hoping your resume will be good enough to catch the employer's attention.

The problem with this mindset is that recruiters typically review the information entered in the application before they view the attached resume. If the information entered in the application is sloppy, incomplete, or not legible, it may impact the recruiter's decision to open the resume, where the real magic happens (e.g., where you highlight how your experience aligns with the job you are applying for).

For example, let's say Joe, a car salesman, is applying for an outside sales job in health care. In the "Position Description, Duties, and Responsibilities" box, he enters: See resume.

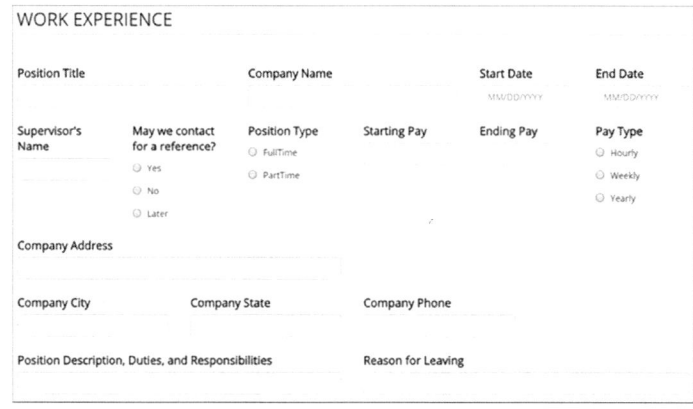

"See resume" is what the recruiter is going to see if they click on his application in the ATS. Since Joe's current position is different from the job title he is applying for, the recruiter may not even bother to open his resume because he may not seem like a great fit on a very surface level.

When filling out an online application, keep in mind that someone will be reading everything you type in the boxes before they open your resume. Make sure what you write is legible, complete, error-free, and does not provide any negative information (i.e., always be professional about your reason for leaving).

Recruiters are busy. They are not going to read more resumes than they have to, so fill out the application in a manner that helps make their jobs easier.

Beware of Parsing

Many applicant tracking systems give you an option to parse your resume, LinkedIn profile, or Facebook account to fill out the online application. While it may save you time, it can be more advantageous to manually complete the application so you can control what the recruiter will see on the other side. Additionally, your other profiles have not been tailored to the job you are applying for like your resume should be.

In spite of the sophistication of ATS parsing capabilities, you cannot count on it to be your cheerleader.

Apply for Jobs like Mad

The longer you wait to apply for a job, the larger the applicant pool will get. People that apply for jobs as soon as they are posted have a better chance of ranking higher in a search because there will be fewer applications to compete with. Ultimately, this means you need to be dedicated to the job hunt and armed to tailor your resume to each job posting as efficiently as possible. It can have a huge payoff.

Read the Application Instructions Carefully

A great way to reduce a large applicant pool is to eliminate applicants that do not follow simple instructions.

If the form tells you to submit your resume in a certain format, follow the instructions. If the form tells you that only candidates with cover letters will be considered, write a cover letter. If you miss following a simple instruction, your application could get thrown out.

When You Are Really Determined

You can do everything right, but that does not always mean your resume will make it to a recruiter. While you always have to formally apply for a job for legal reasons, it never hurts to have a backup plan if you are really interested in a job.

Plan B: If you know someone who already works for the company you are applying at, ask him/her to pass your resume along to the recruiter or hiring manager working on the position.

This strategy works well because referrals are a preferred hiring source. Recruiters will usually consider referrals from internal employees with more weight than people who apply online. Some companies even have a referral bonus.

Plan C: LinkedIn is a great tool when you are job hunting because it truly is the largest professional network in the world.

You can sometimes find the person recruiting for a job you want to apply for by doing a simple search.

- If the job you are applying for is posted on LinkedIn, the person who posted the job (usually someone in recruiting) will sometimes be listed in the job posting in the top right corner of the screen. If you have a LinkedIn Premium account, you can send that person "inmail." Inmail enables you to send a message directly to the inbox of someone you are not connected to on LinkedIn. If you send an inmail to a recruiter, it will go straight to the inbox of the e-mail account linked to their LinkedIn profile. This is a pretty powerful strategy, especially compared to taking your chances in the ATS.

- You can also use LinkedIn to do an advanced people search for "recruiters at company X" to see if you can find the names of the recruiters currently working for the company you are applying at. Most recruiters are active on LinkedIn because they use the site a lot for their job. If you find multiple recruiters at the same company in your search, consider contacting one of them about the job. If they are not working on the position, they may pass your information along to the person who is working on the job.

HOW TO CONTACT DEBRA

Web: www.virtualresumecoach.com
Twitter: https://twitter.com/DebraMastic
Email: debra@virtualresumecoach.com

For customized workshops and materials like *Resumes Made Simple*, please contact Debra.

Made in the USA
San Bernardino, CA
30 August 2018